DISCARDED

D1220931

AROUND THE WORLD IN...

300 B.C.

AROUND THE WORLD IN...
300 B.C.

by Pamela F. Service

BEDFORD PUBLIC LIBRARY
3 MEETINGHOUSE ROAD
BEDFORD, NH 03110

BENCHMARK BOOKS

MARSHALL CAVENDISH
NEW YORK

*With thanks to J. Brett McClain of the Oriental Institute,
the University of Chicago, for his careful reading of the manuscript*

Benchmark Books
Marshall Cavendish Corporation
99 White Plains Road
Tarrytown, New York 10591-9001
www.marshallcavendish.com

Copyright © 2003 Marshall Cavendish Corporation

All rights reserved. No part of this book may be reproduced or utilized in any form
or by any means electronic or mechanical including photocopying, recording, or by any information
storage and retrieval system, without permission from the copyright holders.

• • •

Library of Congress Cataloging-in-Publication Data
Service, Pamela F.
300 BC/Pamela F. Service
p. cm—(Around the world in)
Includes bibliographical references and index.
Summary: Surveys important occurrences in Europe, Africa, Asia, and the Americas 2300 years ago.
ISBN 0-7614-1080-5 (lib. bdg.)
1. History, Ancient—Juvenile literature. [1. History, Ancient.] I. Title. II. Series
D57 .S48 2002   930—dc21   00-036026

• • •

Printed in Italy
1 3 5 6 4 2

• • •

Book Designer: Judith Turziano
Photo Research: Rose Corbett Gordon, Mystic CT

• • •

half title: The Xi'an terra-cotta warriors made for China's first emperor.
title page: A Mayan priest in ceremonial headdress (*left*); a Mayan ballplayer (*right*).

• • •

CREDITS
Front cover: (top left) © The British Museum; (top right) Arthur Thévenart/CORBIS;
(bottom left) Oriental Institute of the University of Chicago; (bottom right) Erich Lessing/Art Resource
Back cover: (top) British Museum, London, UK/Bridgeman Art Library;
(bottom) Francesco Venturi, Kea Publishing Services, Ltd./CORBIS

Page 1: Tomb of Qin Shi Huang Di, Xianyang, China/Bridgeman Art Library; page 2: Mexico City, Museo
Antropologia/Art Resource; page 3: DK Images; pages 6, 38, 41, 83: North Wind Pictures; pages 11, 20: Mary Evans/Edwin Wallace;
pages 12, 29, 43: The Granger Collection, New York; pages 14-15: Museo Nazionale, Napoli/Art Resource; pages 16, 25, 27, 28,
40, 64: Erich Lessing/Art Resource; page 17: Fitzwilliam Museum, University of Cambridge, UK/Bridgeman Art Library;
pages 19, 42: Mary Evans Picture Library; page 23: Drents Museum, Assen, Netherlands; page 24: National Museum of
Ireland, Dublin, Eire/Bridgeman Art Library; page 30: Francesco Venturi, Kea Publishing Services, Ltd./CORBIS;
page 35: Stock Montage, Inc.; pages 36-37: Clore Collection, Tate Gallery, London/Art Resource, NY; page 45: © The British
Museum; pages 47, 49, 71: Werner Forman/Art Resource, NY; page 51: Hutchison Library; page 54: British Museum,
London, UK/Bridgeman Art Library; page 55: Arthur Thévenart/CORBIS; page 59: Dinodia Photo Library; pages 63,
77, 78: Giraudon/Art Resource, NY; page 64: Zhang Shui Chen/Bridgeman Art Library; page 66: © The British Museum;
page 67: Foto Marburg/Art Resource; page 72: Macduff Everton/CORBIS; page 74: SEF/Art Resource, NY;
page 80: Yann Arthus-Bertrand/CORBIS; pages 84-85: Richard A. Cooke/CORBIS; page 86: John Senser.

CONTENTS

Introduction • 7

PART I: EUROPE

THE GREEKS: ALEXANDER THE GREAT CONQUERS THE "WORLD" • 10

THE CELTS: WARRIORS FIERCE AND PROUD SPREAD ACROSS EUROPE • 18

THE ROMANS: ON THE ROAD TO EMPIRE • 26

PART II: AFRICA

THE CARTHAGINIANS: SEAFARERS OF THE MEDITERRANEAN
MAKE THE ULTIMATE SACRIFICE • 34

THE EGYPTIANS: PTOLEMY TAKES COMMAND • 40

THE KUSHITES: KING ARAKAMANI CHANGES TRADITION • 44

THE PEOPLE OF NOK: ARTISTS OF THE FOREST • 48

PART III: ASIA

THE PERSIANS: SELEUCUS BATTLES ANTIGONUS THE ONE EYED • 54

THE INDIANS: A TROUBLEMAKER BECOMES EMPEROR • 58

THE CHINESE: THE RISE OF THE CH'IN • 62

PART IV: THE AMERICAS

THE MESOAMERICANS: PLAYERS WITH LIFE AND DEATH • 70

THE SOUTH AMERICANS: ANCIENT MUMMIES TELL A STRANGE STORY • 76

THE NORTH AMERICANS: WHO WERE THE MYSTERIOUS MOUND BUILDERS? • 82

World Events Around 300 B.C. 88 • Glossary 89
For Further Reading 90 • On-line Information 92
Bibliography 93 • Index 95

An astronomer in
Alexandria, Egypt,
around 300 B.C.,
studies the heavens.

INTRODUCTION

The time is around 300 B.C. On the dry coastal plains of what is now Peru, the Nazca people are covering the ground with a mysterious network of lines that stretch for miles. On the Balkan Peninsula a young Macedonian prince is conquering a wild horse, in preparation for conquering much of the known world. In North Africa a city called Carthage is thriving, growing rich thanks to the skills of its seafaring merchants. To the east, in Asia, small kingdoms that have been at war for centuries are about to unite under the Ch'in—rulers who will give China its name and its identity as a nation. From continent to continent, things are happening.

If you could board a time machine and get off at 300 B.C., these are some of the events you would witness. Most people learn about history by focusing on just one country or place. Most of the time they learn about events only from their own perspective, that is, from the point of view of their nation or heritage. This is certainly a valid way to try to understand the world, but it can also be narrow and one-sided. In this book we thought it might be worthwhile to take a different approach to history, by looking at events that were occurring all across the world at one period of time. Around 300 B.C., for example, Alexander the Great built an empire that played a crucial role in the rise of Western civilization. But civilization and "progress" were happening in other parts of the world, too. Perhaps if we take this broader, "bird's-eye" view of history, all of us may be able to understand one another a little bit better.

So step aboard our "time machine" and get ready to take a trip around the world.

IRELAND

BRITAIN

York

N
W   E
S

Atlantic
Ocean

EUROPE AROUND
300 B.C.

Alps

ETRURIA
(Etruscans)
Tiber R.
Rome

MACEDON

GREECE

Black Sea

Gordium

Issus

Mediterranean Sea

CELTIC LANDS
ALEXANDER'S EMPIRE

Miles   0   100   200   300
Kilometers 0   100   300   500

PART I

EUROPE

In 300 B.C. Europe was nothing like the way it is today. There were no nations as we know them, no big cities, and the culture—the arts, beliefs, and customs of the people—had yet to be fully developed. European civilization was just beginning.

A few years before 300 B.C., in the southern part of the continent, a young man marched out of his small Greek kingdom, gathered armies, and conquered much of what to him was the known world. In the north a people known as the Celts controlled a world of their own, stretching from the British Isles to the Turkish highlands. And on the Italian Peninsula a small city was growing into what a few centuries later would be the most powerful empire in the world.

WHEN THEY RULED
The Greeks
1650 B.C.—146 B.C.

The Celts
800 B.C.—A.D. 796

The Romans
753 B.C.—A.D. 410

THE GREEKS
ALEXANDER THE GREAT CONQUERS THE "WORLD"

Alexander ran ahead of his father, King Philip of Macedon. His sandals slapped along the steep dirt path as he raced to the horse meadows. He wanted to be the first to see the expensive black stallion the horse dealer had brought. When he did, the boy caught his breath. The horse was magnificent.

King Philip and his companions arrived and watched as the horse reared and kicked, refusing to let anyone ride him. Finally the king turned away, disgusted.

"I'm not paying for such a wild, undisciplined beast!"

"What a wonderful horse we're losing," Alexander cried, "just because those men aren't brave or smart enough to handle him!"

"And I suppose you could handle him better than your elders?" Philip scoffed.

"I bet you the price of the horse that I could!"

Everyone laughed, but Alexander ran to the horse. He'd been watching carefully and had noticed that as it pranced about, the stallion seemed spooked by its own shadow. Stroking and talking to the horse, the boy turned it into the sun so that the shadow fell out of sight. Then he leaped onto its bare back.

Philip watched in agony as his son and heir urged the stallion into a wild gallop. But at the end of the field, Alexander expertly turned his mount and rode back in triumph while everybody cheered.

"My boy," the king said through tears of joy, "seek a kingdom to match yourself. Macedon is not large enough to hold you."

Within a few years Alexander the Great did exactly that.

Alexander taming Bucephalus in front of King Philip and his court. This modern illustration captures Alexander's bravery but probably exaggerates the boy's age and the elaborateness of the architecture. Macedon at the time was considered provincial and crude by the rest of Greece.

The story of Alexander's boyhood, recorded when he was twelve, tells how he acquired his horse, Bucephalus. It also shows parts of Alexander's character that never changed. Throughout his life he was competitive, observant, impetuous, and eager for challenges.

Alexander was born in 356 B.C. His country, Macedon, a mountainous region northeast of Greece, shared much of Greek culture, but the Greek

Alexander (left) *and his teacher Aristotle. Aristotle's insistence on rational thinking based on observation inspired some of Alexander's drive to reach new lands and peoples.*

A Knotty Problem

People of Alexander's time believed in prophecies, the idea that gods would give signs about the future. Everywhere he went, Alexander visited temples and asked for divine predictions.

After conquering Gordium, in modern Turkey, he was taken to a temple and shown the chariot of the city's first king. The priests pointed to the intricate knot connecting the pole of the chariot to its yoke and told of a prophecy: whoever could undo the knot would conquer all of Asia.

Ever ready for a challenge, Alexander tried to untie the knot. For half an hour the smug priests and worried soldiers watched. Then, impatiently, Alexander whipped out his sword and cut the knot in two.

Smiling at the shocked priests, he said, "The gods didn't say how the knot was to be undone."

Alexander went on to conquer much of Asia, and he did so in the same unexpected and direct way—by using his wit and the sword.

city-states considered Macedonians uncouth provincials. Nevertheless, Alexander received an excellent education in Macedon's School of Pages, where the sons of nobility were trained to be leaders. There the philosopher Aristotle taught students how to think logically and encouraged them to be curious about the world. There they also learned warrior skills and how to endure hardship.

Alexander had a fiery temper and a superstitious nature, traits he inherited from his mother, Olympias. From his father he inherited a dream—uniting the Greek city-states and leading them to victory against their ancient enemy, Persia.

At the age of eighteen, Alexander got the chance to prove himself. He brilliantly commanded a wing of his father's troops against a Greek army, and after the victory he was given charge of the peace negotiations. From then on, with his knack for innovative strategy and charismatic leadership, the young warrior never lost a battle.

Shortly after Alexander's first victory, however, his father was assassinated. At scarcely twenty years of age, the prince took command of Macedon's army and led his men against warring tribes in the north. After some victories he made treaties with the Celts, whom he called great warriors but also "great boasters." Through war and diplomacy he next united the quarreling Greek city-states under his leadership. Then he took his Macedonian-Greek army, composed now of professional soldiers, across the sea to Asia. There they won their first battle in their war with the Persian Empire.

Before going farther into Persian territory, Alexander "secured his flank." He first captured Tyre and other port cities along the Mediterranean coast so that the Persian fleet could not use them. There were some fierce battles. Some cities in the area, however, had been Greek settlements, and their citizens welcomed Alexander as a liberator from the hated Persians. Next he swept into Egypt and Libya, where he met with hardly any resistance. Egyptians, anxious to end years

Alexander defeating Darius at the battle of Issus. Darius III, Great King of Persia (in chariot at left) lost three battles to Alexander (on horse at right) before being killed by one of his own allies.

of Persian control, greeted the young conqueror as a king and a god.

Alexander next headed eastward, fighting many battles and eventually capturing Persia, Mesopotamia, and present-day Afghanistan. After several victories in northern India, however, his troops called a halt. Alexander wanted to go on—he always wanted to know, and control, what lay beyond the next river or mountain. But his soldiers were tired after years of fighting, and India seemed too big, too hot, and too unfamiliar. What's more, they were terrified of the Indian battle elephants.

By this time Alexander's empire was larger than any the world had known. And in his march across many lands, he had become more than just a conqueror; he had become a ruler as well. His plan was to unite the many different lands into one lasting empire, one that combined the best of the Greek and Asian cultures. With this strategy in mind, he worshipped local gods, married local princesses, added local soldiers to his

This head of Alexander was unearthed in Pergamum, Turkey. Greek artists and the Greek art style spread throughout Alexander's empire. This piece shows the conqueror with god-like beauty combined with an appealing touch of humanity in his wrinkled brow.

A gold coin with the face of Alexander. Following Alexander's conquests, Greek coins became the standard currency in the empire.

army, and even wore local fashions. Everywhere he founded new cities. Many of these were called Alexandria, and one was even named Bucephala after his horse, which died there in battle. To these and older cities, he brought Greek traditions; he built temples, roads, theaters, sports fields, and water systems.

On his return from India, at age thirty-two, Alexander died of fever— or perhaps poison. After some upheaval his empire was divided among his generals. Alexander had never had the chance to turn the conquered lands into the unified, well-run empire of his dreams. By 300 B.C. his generals were fighting among themselves over who would control what territory. Even so, Greek civilization had taken root. Greek coinage, philosophy, and art spread. Centuries later the Christian Gospels were written in Greek because it was the one language all of the "civilized world" could understand.

Indeed, much of the world around 300 B.C. and after was shaped by one man—Alexander, rightly called the Great.

THE CELTS
WARRIORS FIERCE AND PROUD SPREAD ACROSS EUROPE

Seven-year-old Cuchullin sat at dinner with the other boys of the warrior school. Within the thatch and logs of the king's hall, the air was filled with cooking smoke and the sound of singing and laughter. Warriors feasted on roast boar, drank ale, and boasted of their wealth and their deeds in battle. Then, above the clamor rose the voice and harp of the king's bard. He sang of great warriors of the past, of their skill with sword and spear, their red-hazed battle frenzy, and their triumphs in single combat. Cuchullin listened, his eyes sparkling in the torchlight as he dreamed of being a warrior and having his deeds told through all time.

Next morning he and the other boys sat around their teacher, a Druid who understood how this world and the Other World intertwined. In explaining that certain days were considered lucky for certain things, the man said, "Take this day, for instance. Any young boy who takes up arms today will shine in battle and his fame will endure, but his life will be short."

Hearing this, Cuchullin jumped up and cried, "Then I'll go to the king and ask for my warrior's weapons today! I don't care if my life is brief as a flame, so long as my deeds live after me!"

In this ancient Irish legend, the hero Cuchullin might have been speaking for all Celts. Heroic fame was what they valued most. Though in the stories his life was indeed short, Cuchullin's heroic deeds are still told

Cuchullin charges into battle on board his chariot. The Celts' use of the chariot helped them conquer less mobile European peoples.

today. And like him, the Celts left a lasting mark—though their rule ended two thousand years ago.

The Celts had begun as a simple farming tribe in central Europe. But around 800 B.C. they made a momentous discovery; they became among the first Europeans to learn how to work iron. This gave them stronger tools so they could grow more crops and feed more people. And their strong new

A Druid New Year's ceremony. The chief priest carries mistletoe, an evergreen plant that symbolizes eternal life.

CITY OF BOARS

If you have ever dealt with real pigs, you know they can be fat and ornery. But the boars, or wild pigs, of ancient Europe were lean and mean. The Celts admired their fierceness and made them symbols of warrior strength. Certain places were considered sacred to the "orc," as the boar was called in most Celtic languages.

One such place in northeastern England was later conquered by the Romans and, several centuries after that, by the Vikings. Each invader kept some version of the place name and continued using the boar as the town symbol. The city was called York by the time of King Richard III, in the late 1400s. Richard was also the Duke of York and used a white boar on his battle flag. Years later, when English settlers came to America, they named a new place after the old city: New York.

Today, we may not want to call this famous town New Pig City, but the ancient Celts probably would!

iron weapons meant they could more easily defeat neighboring tribes, who used only bronze, a softer metal.

In this way the Celts spread throughout much of Europe and the British Isles. Around 390 B.C. they even moved into Italy and sacked Rome. The Celts loved fighting—with outsiders and among themselves. They were considered such fierce warriors that they were later hired to fight in the armies of Alexander the Great, Hannibal of Carthage, and Ptolemy II of Egypt.

By 300 B.C. the Celtic world was at its height. But even while the Celts held vast territories, there was never any Celtic empire with a single leader.

Each tribe had its own king or queen. And the Celts usually fought as fierce individuals rather than as a disciplined unit with organized strategy.

What united the Celts were their shared customs, religion, and languages. According to their religion, writing was dangerous because it could put sacred knowledge into the wrong hands. So their history and beliefs were passed down in songs sung by bards or in the teachings of their priests, the Druids. Learning all that was needed to become a Druid could take a boy or girl twenty years.

To the Celts, this world and the next were closely linked. Gods and spirits were everywhere, they believed, and by using what we call magic, mortals could connect the two worlds. People believed that after death they would go to a world so like this one that they could even put off paying their debts until they reached it. Instead of building temples, the Celts worshipped their gods at springs or in forest clearings. There they made animal and human sacrifices. They asked the gods of lakes and rivers for help by throwing valuable items into the water.

Unlike the people who lived in southern Europe, around the Mediterranean Sea, the Celts did not live in cities. They were farmers, and because they were so often at war, most Celts lived in or near hilltop forts. Wealth and importance were determined by the number of cattle a family owned. Celtic women had many rights. They could own property, have some say about whom they married, and even become Druids, warriors, or ruling queens.

What did these warlike farmers look like? Most were blond or redheaded. The men liked big mustaches and swept their hair back, stiffening it with lime. Physical fitness was so valued that potbellied men could be fined when their belts needed lengthening. Both men and women loved bracelets,

Modern scientists have reconstructed the features of a girl who once lived in ancient Celtic Holland. Her body was preserved in a peat bog.

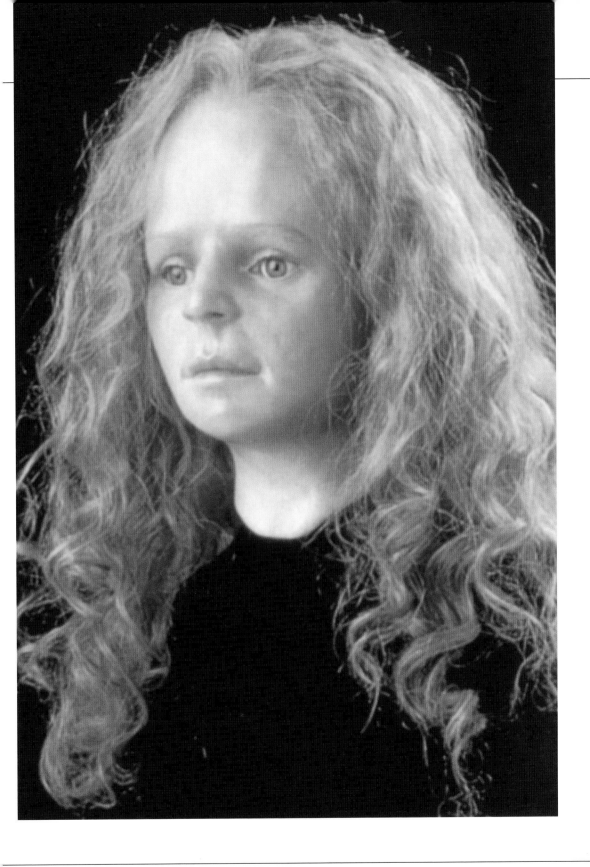

*A golden torque necklace,
found in Ireland. Celts liked to show
off their wealth through jewelry.
Even warriors going otherwise naked
into battle would wear torques.*

earrings, and close-fitting necklaces called torques. Their jewelry, weapons, and all their beautifully made metalwork were adorned with curving, intertwining designs that reflected their belief in the harmony of the natural and spiritual worlds.

In the cold Celtic lands of northern and central Europe, clothes were made of warm wool, often woven into plaids. Women wore long dresses, men wore trousers, and both fastened their cloaks with brooches since there were no buttons. In battle warriors often donned helmets and shields—and nothing else! To demonstrate their fearlessness, the Celts sometimes fought naked except for blue tattoos or body paint.

Even the most fierce warriors, however, would finally prove no match for a united, disciplined army. Rome, the town Celts had looted a century earlier, was growing. In time it would conquer the Celtic lands. Traces of the dynamic warrior culture would remain, however. Even today, two thousand years later, Europe still carries strong echoes of its Celtic past.

This bronze helmet was found in the English river Thames, where it was probably thrown as a sacrifice to the river spirit.

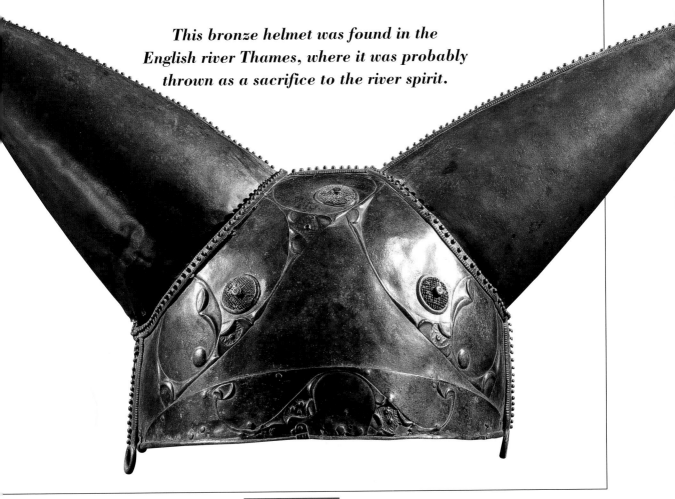

THE ROMANS
ON THE ROAD TO EMPIRE

While the Celts and Greeks were controlling most of Europe, a new power was on the rise. By 300 B.C. Rome had grown from a small village of Latin tribespeople to the most powerful city on the Italian peninsula. In a few more centuries, it would control the largest empire the world had ever known, stretching from Celtic Britain through North Africa and well into Alexander's Asia.

Rome, situated on the Tiber River in central Italy, had once been run by its more powerful northern neighbors, the Etruscans. In 509 B.C., however, the Romans had thrown out the Etruscan kings and established a republic, a more democratic form of government. Not content with just running its own affairs, Rome used wars and alliances to take over neighboring towns. Then it moved north into the Etruscan stronghold and into areas of Italy settled by the Celts. Turning south, it took over the territory of rival tribes and the coastal cities settled by Greeks. Shortly after 300 B.C. nearly all of Italy lay in Roman hands. Rome was ready to face the two major players in third-century Mediterranean politics: Greece and Carthage, a powerful city in North Africa.

What sort of people were these conquering Romans? They were certainly different from the Celts, who glorified the individual and whose territory was a loose grouping of peoples with similar customs. Rome's empire was not like Alexander's either, built on one man's leadership. Instead, its government and military were well organized and efficient enough to outlast one leader or heroic warrior.

Rome's culture was largely borrowed from others. Its architecture, art, theater, and even its gods mostly came from the Etruscans and the Greeks. Rome's strength lay in taking other people's good ideas and making them

Within three centuries of our 300 B.C. date, Rome had reached into Gaul (present-day France). Here a new Roman city with temples and aqueducts nestles in the French Alps.

work better. The idea of democracy, for example, was Greek, but Rome molded it into a government system efficient enough to run an empire.

By 300 B.C. Rome was run by a senate of men from wealthy old families and by an assembly of citizens who were less wealthy. The assembly had the power to turn down senate decisions. The government was administered by two consuls, one elected from each class, who served for terms of one year. This was not a fully democratic system, however, because women and slaves could not vote or seek political office.

One person in the middle of events was Appius Claudius Caecus. He was descended from two earlier officials who had been so tyrannical they had sparked rebellion. But when he was elected in 312 to a powerful government office, Caecus became a reformer and extended voting rights to Romans who didn't own property. He was also a poet and a brilliant engineer. Caecus designed Rome's first aqueduct, a pipeline to carry water into the fast-growing city. The paved road that he had built, the Appian Way, allowed Roman legions to march south and win their wars there. Appius Claudius Caecus was so respected that years later, when he was old and blind, he helped turn the tides of war. Although he had to be carried into

This ancient statue illustrates the legend of Romulus and Remus and the founding of Rome. The twin boys, heirs to a small kingdom, were abandoned along the Tiber River by the man who overthrew their grandfather, the king. A mother wolf nursed them until they were found and raised by a shepherd. In manhood, they fought and put their grandfather back on the throne, then decided to create a city of their own on the Tiber. The two quarreled, and the victor, Romulus, named the city after himself.

WAR ELEPHANTS

*Carthaginian general Hannibal leads elephant
troops against the Romans around 218 B.C.*

Today, armies fear that their enemies will use nuclear or biological weapons. Around 300 B.C. the dreaded secret weapon was, astonishing as it might seem, elephants.

Alexander's army had well-trained warhorses, but they would plunge out of control at the sight and smell of Indian war elephants. Later Pyrrhus, a cousin of Alexander's, imported elephants from India to use in his battles against the Romans. The Romans would face these terrifying living tanks again when they fought the Carthaginians, who brought the elephants from Africa.

The Romans soon learned the trick Alexander had discovered about facing elephants in battle. The beasts might be large and frightening, but if the soldiers aimed at their eyes or shot them with arrows dipped in flaming wax, the elephants would run wild and trample their own troops. The dreaded secret weapon could be made to backfire.

the senate, Caecus made an impassioned speech that motivated the senators to fight on and defeat the last resisting Greek city-state.

Rome's victories depended on more than good roads and fine speeches, however. The Roman army was a first-rate fighting force. As the empire grew, Rome followed Alexander's example and used full-time professional soldiers. Roman soldiers worked as a unit, not as a group of individual warriors, and they fought with the latest technology—siege towers and catapults. The Roman army became the most effective the world had ever seen.

Also, the Romans ruled their vast empire in a new way. The people they conquered were not simply subdued and forced to pay tribute. They were also encouraged to become part of the Roman world, through trade and by gradually adopting its culture and language. In a sense the Roman Empire, though long gone from the map, still exists today. The languages spoken by much of the world, the buildings we live in, and the laws we live under can be traced to that energetic little town on the banks of the Tiber.

Blind and old, Appius Claudius Caecus is led into the Roman Senate, where his speech turns the tide of war.

ROMAN FEASTS

At the height of their empire, centuries after our date, wealthy Romans showed off by holding huge feasts, with rare foods from all over the world. They ate reclining on couches and deliberately stuffed themselves until they were sick so that they could then fit in more food.

The Romans of 300 B.C. would have scorned such decadence. They valued a simple life. Enough good food crops grew in Italy to allow them to enjoy very tasty meals. They had lots of meat, cheese, bread, and vegetables. They cooked with olive oil and ate olives at most meals. And they usually ended their meals with fruit, fresh or dried. Here is a simple dessert recipe, based on one by Apicius, an ancient Roman cook.

STUFFED DATES

30 pitted dates

30 whole shelled almonds

1 small jar of honey

1 cup of crushed cracker crumbs

Carefully cut open one side of each date and put in an almond. Pour the cracker crumbs onto a plate. Warm the honey jar in a bowl of hot water, then pour some honey onto another plate. Roll each date in the honey and then in the crumbs until it is well coated. Place the finished dates on a serving plate and chill in the refrigerator. You can try eating these lying on a couch like a Roman—but the Romans also had bowls of scented water by their places to clean sticky fingers!

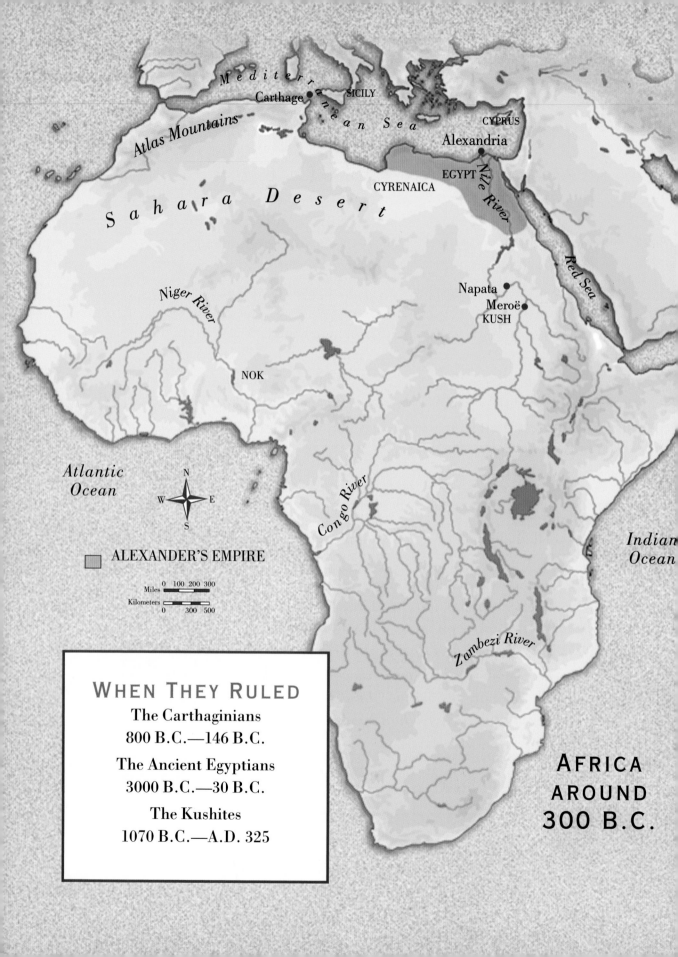

Mediterranean Sea

Carthage ●   SICILY

Atlas Mountains

CYPRUS

Alexandria ●

S a h a r a   D e s e r t

EGYPT

Nile River

CYRENAICA

Red Sea

Niger River

Napata ●

Meroë ●
KUSH

NOK

Atlantic
Ocean

N
W ✦ E
S

Congo River

ALEXANDER'S EMPIRE

Indian
Ocean

Miles   0   100   200   300

Kilometers
0   300   500

Zambezi River

WHEN THEY RULED

The Carthaginians
800 B.C.—146 B.C.

The Ancient Egyptians
3000 B.C.—30 B.C.

The Kushites
1070 B.C.—A.D. 325

AFRICA
AROUND
300 B.C.

PART II

AFRICA

For the last several millennia, the continent of Africa has had a split personality. The split was caused by the vast Sahara Desert. The desert was so difficult to cross that the southern two-thirds of the continent had little contact with the north.

After the invention of writing in Mesopotamia around 3100 B.C., the practice slowly spread to Europe, Asia, and North Africa. People there began recording things about themselves and others. But south of the Sahara, where visits by literate travelers were rare, people did not learn about writing. History happens everywhere all the time, but if it is not written down, it is forgotten. So today, most of what we know about Africa in 300 B.C. is about North Africa.

THE CARTHAGINIANS
SEAFARERS OF THE MEDITERRANEAN
MAKE THE ULTIMATE SACRIFICE

If you could board a time machine and go back to anywhere in the world around 300 B.C., you might want to avoid Carthage. It could be a hazardous place for young people.

Carthage was a powerful city on the northern coast of Africa, noted for its military and economic might. For hundreds of years, however, it was also noted for something else—its practice of child sacrifice.

Carthaginians believed that if they had a particularly important need—if, for example, a war was going badly or disease was spreading—they had to convince their deities of their great devotion. The way they did this was to sacrifice what they valued most—their own children.

Parents would dedicate a newborn baby or even an older child to the god Ba'al Hamon or the goddess Tanit. Then, on a moonlit night, they would take the child to a priest, who would cut its throat and place the body in the arms of a bronze god. From there it would roll into a fire at the statue's feet. To cover up any protest or crying from the parents—so that the gods would not be angry—musicians would play loudly on flutes, lyres, and tambourines. The bones and ashes of the child would finally be placed in a small jar and buried in a special cemetery.

Child sacrifice did not begin with the Carthaginians. It had been practiced earlier by several peoples who lived around the eastern Mediterranean Sea, including the Phoenicians. It was from the Phoenicians' chief city of Tyre that, around 800 B.C., a group of seafarers left and founded Carthage.

In time Tyre abandoned child sacrifice, but Carthage did not. Perhaps the people felt insecure on the colonial frontier and were afraid to anger

A FOUNDING MOTHER

Legend says that Carthage was founded by a very clever woman. Dido was a princess of Tyre, a city on the eastern Mediterranean, in what is now Lebanon. She was the sister of the king of Tyre. When the two quarreled and the king killed Dido's husband, the princess fled by sea along with a small band of supporters. Eventually the refugees landed in North Africa, at a spot with good harbors and defendable hills, where they built a town. They called it Carthage, which meant "new town" in Phoenician.

But the area was not uninhabited. Berber tribes had already made it their home. Iarbus, the local chief, thought that Dido was beautiful, but he did not welcome foreigners taking his land. So he gave Dido an ox hide and said that her people could have as much land as the hide could cover. Cleverly, Dido cut the hide into thin strips and had them laid out to encircle an entire hill. That's where she built her city. Even today, the hill is called Byrsa—the word for "ox hide."

The story of the princess of Tyre and the local Berber king inspired art, literature, and music for centuries afterward. Here Dido is shown marking off her new city of Carthage with strips of ox hide.

the gods. Still, by the fourth century B.C., some Carthaginians were bothered by disapproval from the rest of the "civilized world." They began sacrificing animals or slave children instead of their own offspring, or they bought sacrificial children from the poor.

Around 310 B.C., however, Carthage's long war with the Greek cities

A modern artist's idea of how Carthage may have looked.

on the island of Sicily was not going well. Disease was devastating the Carthaginian army. Sicilian soldiers had landed on the shores of North Africa. Carthage's priests said that all these problems were happening because the gods were angry over receiving such poor sacrifices. They pointed to Tyre, which had given up child sacrifice altogether and had recently been conquered by Alexander the Great. So the Carthaginians tried to make amends by sacrificing a large number of children—five hundred— all at once.

This was a troubled time for Carthage's government as well. The king was advised by a council of elders and by a popular assembly, but often he resented attempts to control his power. In fact, around 360 B.C., King Hanno tried to kill the elders by inviting them to a feast and poisoning their wine. The plot was discovered and Hanno was killed instead, along with all of his relatives, so that they could not avenge him.

Despite the violent practices of the Carthaginians, the city was a center of power and wealth. It owed its success to the skills of its seafaring merchants.

They had explored and traded along the Atlantic coasts of Africa and Europe, and they controlled trade in the western Mediterranean. Carthaginian merchants also ran the caravan routes that crossed the Sahara Desert, bringing gold, ivory, and slaves from central Africa.

In one of the many battles between Rome and Carthage, Roman forces overwhelm a Carthaginian naval vessel.

Carthage itself, covering about fifteen square miles, had splendid buildings and was rich in goods from all over the ancient world.

Carthage was so rich and powerful that, some historians have suggested, it might have become a city of lasting importance. If Carthage had been able to defeat Rome, it would have been the Carthaginians and not the Romans who would have conquered most of the world. Today, many of us would be speaking languages based on Carthaginian instead of Latin. But history did not work out that way.

A few decades after 300 B.C., Carthaginians and Romans would meet in the first of three wars that would last over a century. In the end Rome would destroy Carthage and build on its site another city in the expanding Roman Empire. It would be Rome, not Carthage, that spread its language and civilization throughout much of the world. Perhaps, for the sake of children, that was a good thing.

THE EGYPTIANS
PTOLEMY TAKES COMMAND

When young Ptolemy was going to Macedon's School of Pages with his friend Alexander, he never imagined they would both end up as gods.

Ptolemy accompanied Alexander when he set out to conquer the world and soon became one of his best generals. When Alexander died and control of his empire was being divided up, Ptolemy chose to be governor of Egypt. For years, while the successors to Alexander fought among themselves, Ptolemy kept control of Egypt and Cyrenaica to its west, while periodically winning and losing Palestine, Syria, and Cyprus. Early on, however, it was Ptolemy who snatched for himself the greatest prize of all.

After Alexander's death much time was spent preparing an elaborate funeral carriage and

Ptolemy II and his sister Arsinoë II.

Of the many cities Alexander founded, the one that prospered the most was Alexandria, Egypt. Supposedly, Alexander received a divine vision of this city in a dream and then laid out plans for it.

organizing a procession to carry the conqueror's body from Babylon, his empire's capital, back to Macedon. Ptolemy and his Egyptian army met the procession halfway and kidnapped the body of his old friend. He then built a magnificent tomb in Alexandria, Egypt, where the town's namesake was worshipped as a god.

Egyptians had been worshipping their kings as gods for three thousand years. They believed that when a person became king, he became a form of the god Horus, and when he died he became one with Horus's father, Osiris,

LIGHT OF THE ANCIENT WORLD

Today, lighthouses are familiar sights along coasts. But this was not always the case.

In ancient times people who lived near the Mediterranean spent a lot of time in boats—trading, fishing, or waging war. These were dangerous pursuits. Seafarers could get lost if fog or distance hid the coastline, and ships could run aground on hidden rocks.

When Ptolemy built Alexandria, he wanted his city to become a beacon for culture and trade, so ships had to be able to reach it safely. He ordered the Greek architect Sostratus to build a great lighthouse. Erected on Pharos Island, just outside Alexandria's harbor, it would guide ships even through darkness or fog. When finished, the lighthouse's marble tower was 423 feet high. Its bottom section was square, its middle octagonal, and its top round. On its peak stood a statue of the harbor's divine guardian. The firewood for its beacon was lifted by crane, and the light was reflected by giant mirrors. Grateful mariners reported they could see it thirty miles out to sea.

The ancients considered the Pharos lighthouse one of the Seven Wonders of the World. And today, the science of lighthouse building is called Pharology.

The Pharos lighthouse was more than just a beacon of light to seafarers. It was meant to symbolize Alexandria's role as a beacon of knowledge to the ancient world.

who ruled the underworld. When Ptolemy changed his title from governor to king, he too became a god in the eyes of the Egyptians. Ptolemy was a down-to-earth sort of person, though, and he resisted being treated as divine. But once he died, his son Ptolemy II had him officially declared a god, and the local Greeks as well as the Egyptians began worshipping him.

During his long life, Ptolemy used religion to unite his diverse subjects. He built a new religion around a little-known god called Sarapis, who took the form of a bull. Ptolemy declared that the god's wife was the powerful Egyptian goddess Isis. Worship of these two deities became popular all over the Greek, and later the Roman, world, uniting people of very different backgrounds.

Ptolemy's interests went beyond politics and religion. After all, he and Alexander had studied under a great teacher: the famous philosopher and scientist Aristotle. Ptolemy built the splendid city for which Alexander had drawn up plans. In it, he founded a university and a library that made Alexandria the center for learning throughout the ancient world. He also began constructing a remarkable lighthouse on the island of Pharos.

The Library of Alexandria, reconstructed in this nineteenth-century drawing, was the greatest library in the world until modern times. Its 532,000 scrolls contained Greek knowledge and translations from countries as far away as India.

THE KUSHITES
KING ARAKAMANI CHANGES TRADITION

If you sailed south of Egypt along the Nile around 300 B.C., you would pass some dangerous, rocky stretches and then enter another ancient land, the kingdom of Kush. The Kushites were African people who had taken on many Egyptian ways. Centuries earlier they had even conquered Egypt and ruled it as Egypt's Twenty-fifth Dynasty.

Once they left Egypt, the Kushites no longer believed that their kings were gods. They did believe that their kings could act as divine go-betweens, telling the gods what the people needed and telling the people what the gods wanted in return. The kings of Kush, however, ran into problems with the nation's priests, who thought they had a more direct line to the gods. This dispute was behind a major event in 300 B.C. Kush.

For centuries Amon was the most important god in Kush. His main temple was in northern Kush, near Napata, the kingdom's religious capital. Napata had once been the nation's political capital, but that had been moved south to Meroë (MER-oh-ee) by 300 B.C. It was in Napata that the kings and queens of Kush were crowned and buried.

According to an old tradition, if the priests of Amon felt that a king wasn't doing his job properly, they could order him killed and help choose a new king. So when the priests had a quarrel with King Arakamani around 300 B.C., they decided that he must go. The king, however, decided it was time to change the tradition. He marched his soldiers to the temple of Amon and had the chief priests killed instead.

After that, Arakamani knew he would not be popular with the priests in Napata, so he had the religious capital of the kingdom moved south as well. From then on, the temples around Meroë became more important, and

For centuries, Kush and Egypt had contact through trade and war. This Egyptian tomb painting from 1400 B.C. shows Kushites bringing tribute, including gold and animal skins.

royal burials took place under nearby pyramids.

Meroë made a better capital in many ways. The climate in North Africa had been growing steadily drier, but Meroë was far enough south to remain out of the desert belt. Enough grass grew in the area to support the kingdom's many cattle. Also, Meroë was located near an important resource that

MYSTERIOUS MEROITIC

The Kushites wrote their language, Meroitic, in a hieroglyphic system inspired by the Egyptians. Today, however, that language has been totally forgotten. We can read the characters, but we don't know what the words mean. Someday, perhaps, someone will decipher the language (perhaps someone reading this book!). But until then the mysterious hieroglyphs do make a good secret code.

Here are some Meroitic hieroglyphs and their meaning in our alphabet. The Kushites didn't use all the same letters we do, so some of our letters are left out here and Egyptian hieroglyphs substituted for others. You can use these hieroglyphs to write your name or secret messages that few people—today anyway—can read.

A   G   M   T

B   H   N   U

C   I   O   W

D   J   P   Y

E   K   R

F   L   S

⋮ Word divider

You could write something like this:

(My name is Pam. I write books.)

was missing altogether from Egypt and northern Kush—iron. Iron smelting soon became a major industry at Meroë. Kush had always been noted for its fine archers; now many were armed with iron arrowheads.

As the center of Kush moved from the north to the south, Egyptian influence lessened. Art styles and standards of beauty became more like those we recognize as typically African. Eventually Egyptian hieroglyphs were replaced by a writing system called Meroitic, after the capital at Meroë. Occasionally Kush was ruled by queens, which rarely happened in Egypt or other Mediterranean countries. And to the collection of Egyptian gods that Kush had adopted, the Meroites added some of their own. Chief among these was Apedemek, a fierce warrior god in the form of a lion.

Much of Kush's military activity around 300 B.C., as at other times, was against desert tribes who wanted to move into the rich Nile Valley. The Ptolemaic kings of Egypt generally respected their border with Kush, and after one partial invasion, Rome turned back and left Kush out of its empire. The rocky stretches of river, the desert, and the fierceness of Kush's iron-equipped warriors helped protect the kingdom for centuries more. Credit for the land's strong defense might also be given to the army's practice of training elephants for battle. War elephants were a formidable weapon in ancient times. And no doubt the Kushites would also thank their kings and queens for their national security, for, though not divine, the monarchs could convince the African lion god to take care of his people.

After Kush conquered and ruled Egypt from around 750 to 650 B.C., the Kushite rulers adopted many features of Egyptian royalty, including pyramid burials.

THE PEOPLE OF NOK
ARTISTS OF THE FOREST

An old question goes, "If a tree falls in the woods and no one is there to hear it, does it make a sound?" Another version might be, "If people in the past did things but no one recorded them, do the people have a history?"

The African people living south of the Sahara had a history that was probably as fascinating as the history of Carthage, Rome, or China, but it was not written down so it is hard to appreciate. Archaeology helps, but in the damp African soil not much archaeological evidence is preserved. Still, we do know that around 300 B.C. a people we call the Nok were flourishing near the Niger River in West Africa. They were great artists, making wonderful clay figures of people and animals. Also, they smelted iron and other metals. They may have learned metalworking from trade contacts with Kush or Carthage, or perhaps they invented it on their own.

In Africa, learning how to work iron had the same effect it had in Europe among the Celts. Stronger iron farm tools meant that more crops could be grown and more people fed. And stronger iron weapons meant that this growing population could move into the territory of other people. About the same time that archaeology shows iron use beginning in Africa, the study of languages shows that people speaking an early language group called Bantu were spreading throughout the continent. These people may have been related to the Nok.

It is unfortunate that nobody wrote about the wars and heroes of the Nok people or recorded their hopes and values. It would have made exciting reading. As it is, we can only look at those clay figures crafted by the Nok and wonder what they might have seen.

*The Nigerian people of Nok are known for
their skill in making figures of clay.*

PITS AND PEBBLES

Ancient people throughout the world liked to play games. Toys and game pieces have been found by archaeologists everywhere. In Africa a game called Pits and Pebbles, popular around 300 B.C., was probably also played by the continent's early Iron Age people. But since the game often just uses pebbles and pits scooped in the dirt, it doesn't leave much trace. We know it was played, though, because bored guards around the city of Meroë once ground game pits into the tops of stone walls. Maybe they hid their game playing from their officers—but not from us!

Today, many versions of Pits and Pebbles are played throughout Africa. A few years ago a version of the game, called Mancala, became popular in the United States. You can buy it in a store or make up your own game out of a patch of bare earth and pebbles:

Scratch out two parallel rows of pits in the dirt, with at least six pits on each side. At each end dig a larger pit—the home pits. A player's home pit will be on his or her right side. Put an equal number of pebbles in all the game pits, try four to begin with, using more for more challenging games.

One player sits on each side. Taking turns, a player scoops all the pebbles out of any pit (except the home pit) on his or her side. Then this player drops one pebble into the next pit and each following pit, on both sides (avoiding the opponent's home pit). If your last pebble ends up in your own home pit, you get an extra turn. If your last pebble ends up in an empty pit on your own side, you capture all the pebbles in the opponent's pit opposite and put these in your home pit.

You're not allowed to take pebbles out and count them, so the trick is to figure out which pit has the right number of pebbles to land you in a position that wins more pebbles or more turns. Also, carefully planning where to distribute your pebbles can keep your opponent from winning very many.

The game ends when one side's small pits are empty. The player with remaining pebbles puts them in his or her home pit. The person with the most home pit pebbles wins!

People in modern Sudan (and the rest of Africa) enjoy playing Pits and Pebbles just as their ancestors did thousands of years ago.

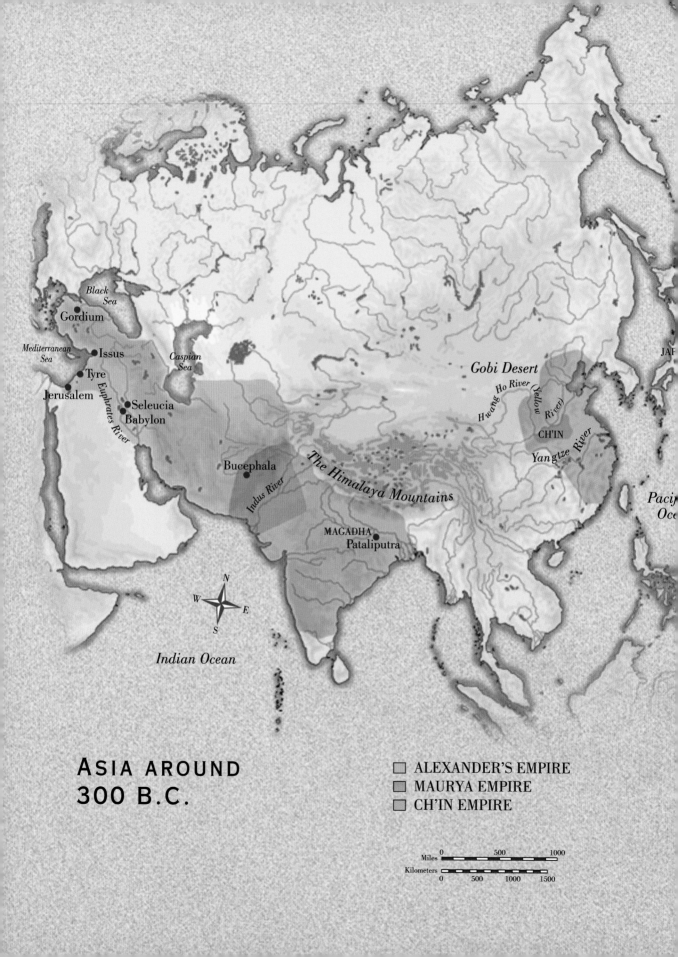

Black
Sea

Gordium

Mediterranean
Sea

Issus

Tyre

Jerusalem

Euphrates River

Caspian
Sea

Seleucia
Babylon

Bucephala

Indus River

The Himalaya Mountains

MAGADHA
Pataliputra

Gobi Desert

Hwang Ho River (Yellow River)

CH'IN

Yangtze River

JAP

Pacif
Oce

N
W   E
S

Indian Ocean

ASIA AROUND
300 B.C.

☐ ALEXANDER'S EMPIRE
☐ MAURYA EMPIRE
☐ CH'IN EMPIRE

Miles   0   500   1000

Kilometers
         0   500   1000   1500

PART III

ASIA

The western portion of Asia was part of Alexander's world. Around 300 B.C. the region was pulled into many of the same events that affected southern Europe and northern Africa. Alexander, however, only went as far as India, and Asia is a vast continent. While the Greek conqueror left an important footnote in Indian history, India was experiencing its own major developments. And beyond the Himalaya Mountains and the bleak deserts of central Asia lay China, its civilization already older than many in the West.

People in various parts of the continent were not ignorant of one another. By ship and overland caravan, goods passed between India, China, and western Asia. Diplomats were exchanged, and adventurers traveled the ancient routes, telling marvelous tales when they returned home. But around 300 B.C. each part of the continent was also experiencing interesting events of its own.

WHEN THEY RULED

The Seleucid Kingdom of Persia
312 B.C.—A.D. 63

The Magadha Kingdom of India
543 B.C.—184 B.C.

The Ch'in Dynasty of China
770 B.C.—210 B.C.

THE PERSIANS
SELEUCUS BATTLES ANTIGONUS THE ONE EYED

That was certainly an extraordinary school, that Macedonian School of Pages which Alexander and his friends attended. It turned out some incredible leaders.

Seleucus, like Ptolemy of Egypt, was a Macedonian who grew up with Alexander and commanded some of his troops. After the conqueror's death Seleucus took control of Babylon, the empire's capital. Soon he was overthrown by a fearsomely named rival, Antigonus the One Eyed. Seleucus fled to Egypt and for years fought in the army of Ptolemy. Finally Ptolemy helped him set up an army of his own, and Seleucus retook Babylon.

He didn't stop there. After years of warfare Seleucus won for

The successors to Alexander also placed their portraits on coins. This silver tetradrachma of Seleucus I was minted in Persepolis (in modern Iran) and looks much like the Alexander coin shown on page 17. Modern nations continue the tradition by placing the profiles of royalty and presidents on their coins.

The ruins of Apamea, the city Seleucus built for his beloved wife.

himself much of Alexander's old empire in Asia. He tried to add India as well, but like Alexander, he was turned back by elephant-mounted warriors. Finally he made a treaty with northern India's strong new king, Chandragupta Maurya. Seleucus gave up claims to India in exchange for five hundred war elephants. This was not as odd a trade as it might seem. India would be very difficult to conquer in any case, and the elephants helped Seleucus win territory he wanted to the west—finally defeating his old enemy, Antigonus the One Eyed.

Seleucus then returned to Macedon, where he and Alexander had started

DIVINE CITY PLANNING

These days, when politicians want to spread their ideas or make themselves look good, they call a news conference. Around 300 B.C. a favorite method used by rulers was to start rumors about their special personal relationship with the gods.

Like Alexander, Seleucus founded many cities, but new things are often hard for people to accept. It helped if stories were spread claiming that a new city was really the idea of the gods.

In Babylon Seleucus was having trouble with the chief priests, who were trying to make themselves more powerful than he was. He decided to build a new city, but he had to work through these same priests to ask the gods what day would be favorable to start construction. Because the priests wanted Seleucus's city to fail, they lied about the answer they received from the gods. Instead of telling him the most lucky day to start construction, they gave him a later date that they thought would be very unlucky.

Someone, however, leaked the truth to Seleucus. He then told his workmen to start early and to spread the story that they had been inspired directly by the gods to begin building on the most favorable day of all. He called the city Seleucia. This wasn't as boastful as it sounds since many leaders of the time named cities after themselves or after friends and relations.

Another time Seleucus was trying to decide where to build a new city. He had just defeated Antigonus the One Eyed and destroyed his city, Antigonia. The people who had lived there were understandably upset, but Seleucus wanted them to like his new city. So he spread the story that when he'd asked the god Zeus where he should put the city, an eagle had suddenly swooped from the sky and flown off with the meat he'd offered as a sacrifice. Seleucus claimed that he'd then leaped onto his horse and chased after the eagle until it dropped the meat on the perfect site for his new city. Who could argue with a choice of the gods?

out many years earlier. He planned to make himself king there as well. But somebody else shared the same ambition. Ptolemy had several sons, one of whom had quarreled with his father and fled Egypt. This young man went to Seleucus's court and behaved as if he were his friend. One day the two went riding together and the younger Ptolemy stabbed Seleucus to death. He then made himself king of Macedon.

Still, despite its tragic end, Seleucus's life had been long and successful. He was popular with his army and his subjects. He was devoted to his wife, Apama, the daughter of a well-liked Persian leader, and named many cities after her. In fact, Seleucus founded a great many cities, and they helped set the roots of Greek civilization deep into Asian soil. His family ruled much of the old Persian Empire as the Seleucid dynasty, until it, too, was swept into the empire of Rome.

THE INDIANS
A TROUBLEMAKER BECOMES EMPEROR

Usually kids who are outspoken and rude get themselves into a lot of trouble. Sometimes, though, these are the very traits that help them get ahead. That's what happened in the case of Chandragupta Maurya.

Chandragupta was the son of an important family in the northern Indian kingdom of Magadha. Apparently, when a teenager, he'd said something insolent to the king, who became so angry that he banished him. Then, according to another story, Chandragupta met the invading Greek army and was so insolent to Alexander that he barely escaped with his life.

Still, the boy was impressed with Alexander. Here was a young leader with vision and energy who had united dozens of states into a single empire. Perhaps, Chandragupta thought, he could do the same. For a while he hid in the forests, forming an army out of mercenaries, rebels, and thieves. He then conquered Magadha, overthrowing the king who'd had him exiled.

When word came that his role model, Alexander, had died, Chandragupta led his army against the Greek garrison and took back the Indian land that Alexander had conquered. He then marched east and south, conquering many small states. By around 300 B.C. Chandragupta Maurya had made himself the first emperor of India, founding the Maurya dynasty.

It was Chandragupta who led elephant-mounted troops against Seleucus, discouraging for many centuries any Westerners who might be thinking of conquering India. Seleucus respected the Indian emperor. Their peace treaty not only exchanged land for elephants. Seleucus also sent his daughter Bernice to be Chandragupta's wife. She may

Few remnants of Chandragupta's time remain, but this depiction of Chandragupta II shows something of the grand court his namesake must have had. Chandragupta I made such an impression on Indian history that this later king adopted his name when founding his own dynasty some six hundred years later.

have been the mother of Bindusara, India's next emperor.

As time passed, the two families remained close and exchanged gifts. Once Bindusara wrote and asked for figs, raisin wine, and a Greek philosopher. Antiochus, Seleucus's son, replied that he would send the figs and the wine but that Greeks didn't trade in philosophers.

The two courts also exchanged diplomats. Seleucid ambassadors were astonished at the magnificence of the Mauryan court. They reported that

INDIAN PILAU

Rice was and is the main food of southern Asia. Poor people ate it plain or with a few vegetables. Chandragupta's court would have enjoyed it in many ways, including this spicy fruit pilau.

2 cups water
$1/8$ teaspoon salt
$1/4$ teaspoon turmeric
1 tablespoon cardamom seeds
1 tablespoon coriander seeds
1 cup uncooked rice

$1/2$ teaspoon cinnamon
$1/4$ teaspoon nutmeg
1 cup dried fruit—raisins, apples, dates, apricots, pears, or, Bindusara's favorite, figs
1 tablespoon dried mint

Bring the water to boil in a saucepan, then add the salt, turmeric, cardamom seeds, and coriander seeds. Now add the rice. Cover the pan and let it simmer for twenty minutes. When the water is absorbed, add the cinnamon, nutmeg, and dried fruit (whole or cut into small chunks). Stir, place in an elegant serving bowl, and sprinkle with dried mint.

the capital city, Pataliputra, was nine miles long and one and a half miles wide. The king's huge palace had carved wooden pillars covered in gold and was set in lush gardens where peacocks, parrots, and pheasants strutted. The royal children swam and sailed their toy boats in the fishponds.

The ambassadors described courtiers sparkling with jewelry and wearing flowered robes embroidered in gold. When the king left the palace, he rode an elephant bedecked with gold and pearls. The favorite royal sports were hunting and watching wild beasts fight each other in the arena. The king was guarded by women warriors who had been bought as children and raised to be loyal only to the king. Even so, to avoid assassination, the king slept in a different room each night. The court feasted on richly spiced foods served in golden bowls and drank from golden goblets set with gems.

For a boy who got into trouble, Chandragupta and his family ended up pretty well.

THE CHINESE
THE RISE OF THE CH'IN

The period around 300 B.C. was a troubled time for the Chinese. It was toward the end of what historians call the Period of Warring States.

For several thousand years people had been farming and building cities in China's rich river valleys. They had learned to work bronze and iron and to create beautiful art in styles that were distinctly Chinese. They had also developed their own writing system, which was very different from those used in the West. During periods when one strong state dominated several weaker ones, there was little warfare.

But in the eighth century B.C., the powerful state of Chou started to disintegrate. Dozens of smaller states began fighting one another, with each king wanting to found China's next ruling dynasty. This warfare went on for hundreds of years, but one state seemed particularly determined to win—the state of Ch'in (sometimes written Qin).

The kings and royal advisers of Ch'in organized their whole society so that they could conquer others. To build a strong, well-fed population, they forced people to leave the towns and work in the countryside, growing food. When the Ch'in conquered other states, they didn't rule through local leaders the way the Chou had done. Instead, they appointed people who were loyal only to the king of Ch'in.

Ch'in's rulers even tried to break down the strong Chinese family system by punishing all the relatives if one family member committed a crime. They rewarded people who informed on wrongdoers and had very severe punishments for even minor crimes. They also standardized the writing and measuring systems used in different regions.

Earlier, warfare in China had been considered almost an art form,

Ch'in Shih Huangti ended the long Period of Warring States and became China's first emperor.

with small groups of nobles fighting under rules of honor and chivalry. The Ch'in, however, drafted thousands of peasants into armies where the chief rule was to win. Around 300 B.C., after many bloody victories, Ch'in defeated the last of its rivals, and in 221 B.C. the king of Ch'in declared

The first Chinese emperor insured his importance even after death. Ch'in Shih Huangti's tomb, discovered in 1974, contains over 6,000 life-sized clay figures of soldiers and horses, meant to protect their ruler in the afterlife. Each soldier was modeled individually with different hairstyles, clothing, and facial features. The tomb reveals not only the power of the Ch'in ruler but also the great skill of ancient Chinese artists.

himself China's first emperor. The name "China" comes from this first imperial dynasty.

The long Period of Warring States had been very troubling to the Chinese. During this time many different schools of thought had sprung up to explain why the world worked as it did and how people should behave. Some of these ways of thinking persisted and became philosophies that are still followed today.

The philosopher Lao-tzu taught that there was a universal balance and order in all things—the Tao, or "Way." People could be happy, he believed, only if they lived in harmony with the natural order. If human laws or customs broke that harmony, they should not be obeyed. Paying reverence to one's ancestors and to the spirits that governed nature and human activities could also help in following the Tao. So could giving up worldly concerns and focusing on one's inner being through meditation.

Another philosopher, Confucius, also believed in the Tao, but he thought the best way to reach it was to follow strict principles for right living. His rules laid out the proper behavior for all members of society, from the king to the youngest child. Each person had a fixed place in society determined by his or her gender and occupation. Confucius taught that everyone

REALITY CHECK

The story goes that the Taoist philosopher Zhuangzi once woke up and told his friends that he had dreamed he was a butterfly floating in a sunny meadow. Then he began to wonder if perhaps he was really a butterfly dreaming he was the philosopher Zhuangzi. Finally he decided it didn't really matter because the only thing that was really "real" was the Tao.

YIN-YANG

The yin-yang symbol, a circle with an S curve dividing light and dark halves, is today seen on everything from pendants to posters. It comes from China and expresses a belief common to Taoism and Confucianism—a belief in eternal balance.

Yin represents all that is dark, passive, and female. Yang stands for what is light, active, and male. Neither one dominates the other. They are in balance, with each containing a small dot of the other.

This is not the concept of Good versus Evil or Light versus Dark that is found in many Western religions. Both yin and yang are needed for harmony. They are the sunlit and the shadowed side of a hill—neither can exist without the other. Evil only comes about when yin and yang fall out of balance. People following this belief need to be calm, moderate, and balanced in all things. But that is not easily done. So having the yin-yang sign around was—and is—a helpful reminder.

In this painting, three teachers are instructing a boy in the meaning of yin-yang and the importance of balance in all things.

should accept their position, obey those in superior positions, and protect those in lesser ones. If people behaved properly toward one another and honored their ancestors, Confucius believed, happiness and order would naturally follow. There would then be little need for laws or wars.

The rulers of Ch'in rejected both schools of thought. They followed a philosophy called Legalism. Unlike the Taoists and Confucianists, they thought that people were basically evil and that government needed strict laws and harsh punishments to make them behave. Whenever they captured another state, Ch'in leaders burned books of philosophy and history. They also executed philosphers and teachers whom they disagreed with —sometimes burying them alive!

The Ch'in dynasty was not popular and did not rule for long. But its ideal of a strong, united government lasted in China for over two thousand years.

Lao-tzu, founder of Taoism. He is considered one of the most important philosophers in China's long history.

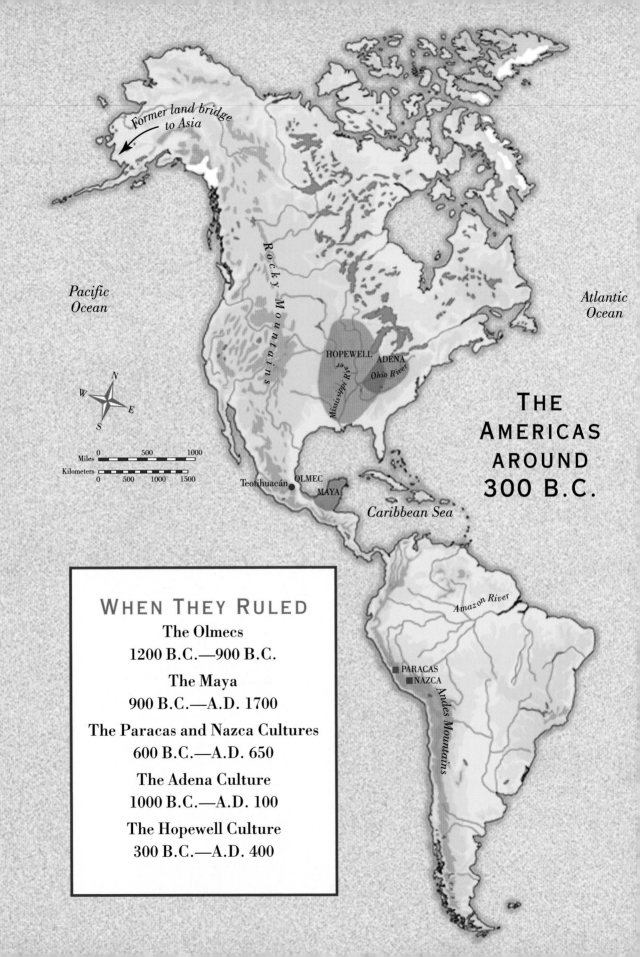

Former land bridge to Asia

Pacific Ocean

Rocky Mountains

HOPEWELL

ADENA

Ohio River

Mississippi River

Atlantic Ocean

THE AMERICAS AROUND 300 B.C.

N
W   E
S

Miles   0   500   1000
Kilometers   0   500   1000   1500

Teotihuacán   OLMEC

MAYA

Caribbean Sea

Amazon River

PARACAS

NAZCA

Andes Mountains

WHEN THEY RULED

The Olmecs
1200 B.C.—900 B.C.

The Maya
900 B.C.—A.D. 1700

The Paracas and Nazca Cultures
600 B.C.—A.D. 650

The Adena Culture
1000 B.C.—A.D. 100

The Hopewell Culture
300 B.C.—A.D. 400

PART IV
THE AMERICAS

Twenty-five thousand years ago the world was in the grip of an ice age. It was so cold that around the poles the ocean water froze, causing sea levels everywhere to drop. Places that had been underwater emerged as dry land. In northeast Asia hunters following caribou or other game eastward crossed one of these land bridges. Without knowing it, they had entered a new world.

When the Ice Age ended, the land connection disappeared, but the new arrivals kept spreading south into richer and warmer lands. Around 5000 B.C. some of them, like their distant relations in the Old World, learned how to plant crops and stop wandering after food. This meant that more people could stay together in fixed places, which required more organized living. Governments and religions arose, and palaces and temples replaced chief's huts and simple shrines. Civilization had begun in the Americas.

THE MESOAMERICANS

PLAYERS WITH LIFE AND DEATH

One day, when the world was young, twin brothers found their father's ballplaying equipment. Excitedly, they strapped it on and ran out to practice in the stone ball court. They played very well but very noisily. This angered the Lords of Death, who lived under the ground, so the lords challenged the boys to come down and play a match.

The clever twins managed to escape every trap the lords laid for them and played so well that their many games ended in draws. Finally the twins allowed themselves to be killed, but magically they came back and tricked the Lords of Death into giving up some of their power over the living. The boys then revived the body of their father, whom the lords had killed earlier and buried under the ball court. Their father became the God of Corn, bringing food to the people. The Hero Twins became gods as well, and the tale of their wondrous ballplaying was told and reenacted for centuries to come.

In Mesoamerica (meso means "middle"), the story of the Hero Twins was popular centuries before our 300 B.C. date. So was playing ball. The Olmec people, who lived in what is now southern Mexico, built large ball courts in their towns. The games they played were both sport and religious ritual.

The Olmec were skilled stoneworkers. Using only stone tools and no metal, they carved beautiful figures out of jade. They also hauled huge

The Olmec were the first people in Mesoamerica to leave major evidence of themselves in stone. This giant head probably represented a god or ruler.

boulders across many miles, using logrollers, rafts, and a great many people, since they had no wheels or pack animals. From these boulders they carved giant stone heads, probably representing their gods or kings. The Olmec were wealthy traders and were the first Americans to develop a writing system and a calendar. But by 300 B.C. their power was fading.

At the same time the power of the Maya, their neighbors to the southeast, was growing. Mayan territory covered what is now the Yucatán Peninsula

The remains of a Mayan ball court and pyramid. Getting the
ball through the stone ring was the goal of the game.

of Mexico plus Guatemala, Belize, Honduras, and El Salvador. By 300 B.C. they were on their way to becoming one of the grandest civilizations of ancient America.

Mayan cities were large and impressive, featuring stone pyramids, palaces, temples, plazas, and, of course, ball courts. Around the cities were farms where the Maya practiced "slash-and-burn" agriculture. Farmers would burn a section of forest and, in the soil enriched by the ashes, plant corn and beans. In a few years the thin forest soil would give out, so the farmer would abandon the field, letting it grow back to forest, and plant a new one. The system worked for centuries until the demand for farmland grew faster than new forests could replenish the soil.

Like the ancient Greeks, the Maya were a collection of small states that often fought one another. But they had no Alexander to unite them. There were times when one kingdom was more powerful than others, but there was never a Mayan empire.

In Mayan belief the World Tree had its roots in the underground land of ancestral spirits. It passed through our world and spread its branches into the starry home of the gods as the Milky Way. The gods and people were interconnected. People believed that if they praised the gods and offered them sacrifices, the gods would tend to their needs.

The king was also the chief priest, and one of his main duties was to carry out religious ceremonies. He and others could get the attention of the deities by deliberately cutting themselves and letting out some of their own blood. This practice could also make a person feel faint and see visions.

Another way to get the gods' attention was to sacrifice valuable items or, for even better results, sacrifice a life. Mayan myths like the one of the Hero Twins showed that life comes out of death the way corn springs from seemingly lifeless seed. So in asking the gods for a better life, the Maya felt they should offer life as well.

At times a king would sacrifice some of his own subjects, but war captives were considered the perfect sacrifice, because by being warriors they had

In this Mayan wall painting, prisoners of war are about to be sacrificed. The most worthy sacrifices were brave warriors captured in battle.

proven themselves brave and so were worthy offerings to the gods. The need for a constant supply of fresh captives to offer the gods may have been one reason the Mayan kingdoms so frequently fought one another. Sacrifices were made in the temples or in the ball court. Captured warriors were forced to play a ball game at the end of which they would lose—the game and their heads.

Not all Mayan ball games, however, were rituals ending in death. Some were simply sport. Players on two teams, wearing leather padding, tried to get a hard rubber ball to opposite goals or through hoops. The rules allowed players to use hips, elbows, or knees but not hands or feet. The ball could be bounced off the steep stone sides of the court but had to be kept off the ground. Spectators loved to bet valuables on a game. Afterward they would quickly scatter, because the winning players had the right to snatch whatever jewelry or clothing they wanted from the fans.

The Maya were more than sportsmen, warriors, and builders. Their priests studied the movements of the stars and planets, accurately predicted eclipses, and developed several types of calendars, which were as accurate as those we use today. They also developed an effective system of mathematics and expanded on the Olmec writing system. Their writing was not alphabetical but used a large number of symbols that stood for words, sounds, or groups of sounds.

The Maya took history very seriously and wrote mainly to record dates

DRINKING MONEY

The ancient Mesoamericans didn't use coins to exchange for goods. Instead, they traded goods among themselves and with people who lived a great distance away. The cacao bean was a particularly valued trade item, and since it was also small and easy to carry, it came to be used as a form of money. Some traders, however, tried to cheat their customers by purchasing goods with beans that they had hollowed out and filled with dirt. To be safe, people had to bite their bean-money to see if it was the real thing.

Cocoa is made from cacao, and then as now it was a favorite drink. But because the beans were also money, only the wealthy could afford to drink it. That was one way people showed off how wealthy they were—by grinding up their money and having a nice hot cup of cocoa.

and events during the reigns of their kings. They carved these accounts into their stone monuments and wrote them in books. Most of these books were later destroyed by the Spanish when they conquered the Maya, but today scholars are learning how to read the remaining inscriptions.

Mayan civilization dominated Mesoamerica for many centuries after our 300 B.C. date, and ballplaying remained an important activity throughout that time. Inscriptions from later years record a king named Eighteen Rabbit who, among his other building projects, reconstructed a large ball court in his city of Copan. History also records that this king was captured in war and lost the game and his life in his enemy's ball court.

In myth and life the Maya took their ballplaying very seriously.

THE SOUTH AMERICANS
ANCIENT MUMMIES TELL A STRANGE STORY

Around A.D. 1200 the land of Peru would give rise to the golden empire of the Incas. But centuries earlier, around 300 B.C., several groups of people in that area had already developed significant civilizations. Like the Maya and Olmec of Mesoamerica, they were farming people who built cities and pyramids of stone and brick and supported skilled artisans. But unlike the Maya, these ancient Peruvians had no writing, and their civilization died out before Europeans came and reported about it. So all we know of them comes from archaeology. Still, theirs is an interesting—and a mysterious—story.

The Paracas people, who lived in Peru's dry mountains, are perhaps best known today for their mummies. When we think of mummies, we usually think of ancient Egypt, but the Paracas also used mummification to preserve the bodies of their dead. Like the Egyptians, they first removed the internal organs, but they didn't use salt baths or ointments to dry out the body, relying instead on the dry desert air. And rather than stretching out the body in a mummy case, they put it in a sitting position and wrapped it in yards and yards of fabric until it became a cone-shaped bundle. This was then put in a large basket and buried.

When excavated, these mummies, particularly their skulls, tell us a great deal about the Paracas. Like many of the peoples who lived in the Americas, the Paracas followed, what seems to us, a strange tradition. They reshaped the heads of infants so that as they grew the children would develop sloping foreheads. The long forehead seems to have been considered a sign of beauty by the Paracas. The skulls that have been found also show that the Paracas had skilled doctors who practiced a delicate medical operation—one that would not be practiced as successfully until modern times. The

aim of the surgery was to relieve concussions, which were caused
by blows to the head with war clubs—the Paracas's favorite weapon.
Like the Maya the Paracas fought many wars, with one aim being to
take prisoners to use as religious sacrifices.

Another thing the mummies tell
us is that the Paracas were
amazingly skilled weavers.
The cloth wrapped around
the bodies was also well
preserved in the dry climate,
and the bright woven and
embroidered patterns show
lively designs, with people,
animals, and geometric
figures. Today, theirs is
considered among the
finest cloth made any-
where in the world at
any time in history.

Around 300 B.C.

*This mummy
from a Paracas
bundle burial
was sent to the
afterlife wrapped
in beautifully
woven cloth and
wearing massive
gold jewelry.*

The Paracas people wove colorful cloth that is still considered
some of the finest in the world. This piece, beautifully preserved
in the dry Peruvian climate, shows mythical winged figures.

the Paracas civilization was coming to an end, but in Peru's coastal deserts another civilization, the Nazca, was getting started. The Nazca buildings and the designs they used on cloth and pottery were similar to the Paracas's. But today, the Nazca are particularly known for something else: they made lines.

On the dry plains along Peru's coast, where the Nazca fished and irrigated fields of corn and potatoes, they also covered the ground with a network of lines. These lines could stretch for miles or they could make up a geometric pattern or the figure of an animal.

Sighting between poles, the Nazca laid cords over the dry, stony ground to plot their remarkably straight lines. Then, along these lines, they removed the dark, weathered stones, exposing the light ground underneath. Today, thousands of years later, the lines are still visible in the nearly rainless desert, but their purpose remains a mystery.

Some scientists studying the lines believe they are essentially a huge astronomy book. Many lines point to spots on the horizon where the sun or certain stars rise at important times of the year. For farming people, who need to know when to plant and harvest, such celestial calendars would have been important. The animal figures drawn on the desert may have represented Nazca gods or perhaps constellations of the zodiac, which varied with the season.

But not all the lines and figures seem to line up with things in the sky. Another possible explanation for some lines is that they were paths leading to sacred places—hills or springs or piles of rock where spirits were thought to live. On their way to these sacred places, people may have thought that by keeping to the straight path they would be safe from any hostile spirits roaming the desert wilderness.

One remarkable thing about the lines, particularly those forming geometric or animal shapes, is that the patterns are almost invisible from the ground. Scientists only began studying them when airplanes made it possible to recognize whole patterns. To some people, this suggests that the drawings were offerings or messages to the gods, who could look down on them from the sky.

Other people have even suggested that the lines were made by or for space aliens. The drawings, they argue, are coded messages, and the lines and long bare rectangles are instructions and landing strips for UFOs. Scientists have pointed out, however, that aliens intelligent enough to build interstellar space-ships wouldn't need anyone to draw landing instructions for them on flat plains!

Besides, the idea that any difficult or mysterious achievements in the past must be the work of aliens is insulting to human beings. Even with limited technology we have done some remarkable things in our past. Learning about and taking pride in those achievements is what history is about.

This desert plain in coastal Peru was a massive drawing board for the ancient Nazca people. The spider figure was made from one continuous line or path.

PIGS OF ANCIENT PERU

Guinea pigs, the modern pet or experimental animal, have a long history with human beings. Their ancestors, the cavies, lived wild in South America. By 300 B.C. ancient Peruvians had domesticated them. They kept a few as pets, but mostly they raised the animals for food.

When it came to livestock, the people of the New World weren't as well provided as those of the Old. There were far fewer animals suitable for domestication. Modern horses, cows, pigs, and sheep first came to America with the Spanish in the 1500s. Until then, the native Americans made do with what they had. In Peru this meant raising llamas, ducks, and guinea pigs.

Guinea pigs, of course, are not pigs, but are rodents like mice or beaver. The Europeans probably called them pigs because these animals are fat and tend to grunt and squeak. They aren't even from Guinea, which is in Africa. Possibly when these animals were first brought to Europe, people mixed up the name Guiana, a region in South America, with the better-known African country Guinea.

Still, though twice misnamed, these little animals were among the few native Americans who clearly benefited from the coming of the Europeans. When bigger, meatier animals like the cow, sheep, and pig were introduced, the guinea pig was no longer needed for dinner. Most could then live in the wild or enjoy the luxurious life of a pet.

Even without knowing how to write, the people of ancient Peru left us an interesting story—partly a mystery story. Perhaps in time we will learn how to read more of that story.

THE NORTH AMERICANS
WHO WERE THE MYSTERIOUS MOUND BUILDERS?

When Thomas Jefferson was a boy, he loved exploring the woods of Virginia and climbing the earthen mounds that rose mysteriously among the trees. Bright and observant even then, Jefferson noticed that some of the trees crowning the mounds were very old. He deduced that the mounds must have been built centuries earlier, and he wondered who had constructed them and why.

When he grew up, Jefferson, who would become the third president of the United States, continued to be curious. In 1784, he decided to make a thorough exploration of one of the woodland mounds. Using techniques surprisingly like those archaeologists work with today, he sliced through a mound, recording everything that was revealed.

He discovered that the little hills were burial mounds made by Native Americans. They were not—as some people believed—built by wandering Egyptians or other ancient foreigners. Interestingly, he found that the mound he excavated was not just a single burial place, but had been used over time, growing increasingly taller as new bodies were added. And since treasure items were buried with the dead—jewelry, pipes and stone tools—Jefferson decided that these early Native Americans must have believed in an afterlife.

Since Jefferson's time scientists have learned more of the mounds' secrets. Around 300 B.C. the Adena people lived in the Ohio River valley. When an important person among them died, he was buried along with some of his treasures in a wooden hut that was then covered with earth. Over time the bodies of other members

This great earthen mound was built by the Adena people in stages, from around 250 B.C. to 150 B.C. Known as the Grave Creek Mound, it is located in West Virginia and is the largest of the Adena mounds. It measures 69 feet high and 295 feet in diameter and took more than 60,000 tons of earth to build.

Forests eventually grew over the ancient mounds. Today scientists are trying to learn their secrets. This aerial photograph shows Ohio's Serpent Mound outlined by a path for modern visitors. The tail of the serpent is coiled while the mouth is open, ready to swallow an egg.

of his group might be added, until the mound rose as high as seventy feet.

Some Adena mounds, however, had few if any burials in them. These were built in geometric or animal shapes. As with the Nazca lines, their true patterns can only be seen from above and their purpose remains a mystery. But the Adena must have had strong reasons for doing what they did, because to construct just one mound required many people hauling thousands of basketfuls of dirt.

The Adena lived by hunting and collecting wild plant food. They also did a small amount of farming. They traded goods over great distances—copper from the Great Lakes and volcanic obsidian from what is now Yellowstone National Park. They also

BOILING WITHOUT POTS

After the Adena began making pottery, other North Americans learned this valuable skill. Before they had pots, early Native Americans mostly barbequed their food. But this meant that the fat dripped into the fire, losing valuable calories needed to survive. Boiling meat and vegetables in pots kept the fat and vitamins in the broth.

Not all native North Americans used pots. Most California tribes never made pottery. Their beautifully made baskets served all the purposes of a pot; they could even be used for boiling food. Cooking baskets were tightly woven of plant fibers that swelled when wet, closing any gaps. The basket was filled with water, and the crushed acorns or other foods were dropped in. Rocks were then put into a nearby fire, and when they got hot were plucked out with wooden tongs and dropped into the basket. Someone had to keep stirring so that the rocks would boil the food but not burn a hole in the basket.

These baskets from California's Miwok Indians were woven tightly enough to be used for cooking.

wove beautifully patterned cloth, and for some of their leaders made capes studded with freshwater pearls. And they were the first North Americans to make pottery.

Around our 300 B.C. period, another group, the Hopewell, were beginning to spread through a larger area of the Midwest and the South. They were wealthier than the Adena, growing more corn and burying their dead with more elaborate items. In time they would be replaced by others who built walled towns and earthen platforms for their temples and houses. Altogether, Mound Builders lived in parts of North America for 2,500 years.

Today, many of their hills have been lost under housing developments and plowed fields. But enough remain to excite the curiosity of new "Thomas Jeffersons," people who may discover even more secrets of the mysterious mounds.

WORLD EVENTS AROUND 300 B.C.

390—Celts sack Rome
356—Alexander the Great born in Macedon
336—Alexander succeeds his assassinated father, Philip
333—Alexander defeats Persian king Darius at Battle of Issus
326—Alexander extends empire to Indus River
323—Ptolemy I founds Ptolemaic dynasty in Egypt
   —Alexander dies in Babylon
322—Chandragupta founds Maurya dynasty
312—Roman leader Appius Claudius Caecus completes Appian aqueducts
       and begins the Appian Way
310—Mass child sacrifice takes place in Carthage to gain gods' favor in war with Sicily
307—Ptolemy I founds library and university at Alexandria
305—Ptolemy I declares himself king
305—Chandragupta defeats Seleucus
301—Seleucus defeats Antigonus the One Eyed at Battle of Ipsus
300*
   —Culture of Paracas people (makers of exquisite textiles) declining
   —Rise of Nazca people (makers of mysterious lines in desert)
   —Olmec civilization declining
   —Mayan civilization on the rise
   —Mexican city of Teotihuacán being settled
   —Decline of Adena culture (Mound Builders who hunted, gathered,
       and did limited farming)
   —Beginning of Hopewell culture (farming Mound Builders)
   —Celts build hill forts and make beautiful metalwork in much of
       central and northern Europe
   —King Arakamani completes move of capital of Kush from Napata to Meroë
   — Sub-Saharan Iron Age under way
   —West African Nok people make clay sculptures
295—Rome defeats the Etruscans
293—Rome defeats Samnites
275—Rome conquers Greek cities in Italy
275—Ptolemy II completes Pharos lighthouse
264—Beginning of First Punic War between Carthage and Rome
221—Centuries-long Period of Warring States in China ends with founding of Ch'in dynasty

*dates approximate

GLOSSARY

bard In traditional European societies, a singer, tale-teller, and keeper of spoken history.

caravan A group of people who travel together.

catapult A military device for mechanically hurling large objects at the enemy.

celts (KELTS) An ethnic group once dominant in much of Europe, now primarily in Scotland, Wales, Ireland, and Brittany, France.

charismatic (kar-iz-MAT-ik) Having a special charm or appeal that attracts people and inspires loyalty.

city-state An independent political unit consisting of a city and the surrounding territory that it controls.

consecutive Items following one after the other in order, with no gaps.

decadence (DEH-keh-dense) The state of being decayed from a higher standard, morally corrupt, or self-indulgent.

Druid A Celtic priest.

dynasty (DIE-neh-stee) A ruling family, or the period of history when that family ruled.

hieroglyphics (hi-row-GLIFF-iks) A writing system in which pictures or symbols stand for words or sounds.

Macedon (MASS-a-don) An ancient land northeast of Greece.

meditation A mental state in which the mind is cleared of petty thoughts and focuses on larger matters or attitudes.

mercenaries (MUR-sin-air-eez) Soldiers who will fight for any army or cause that will pay them; hired foreign soldiers.

millennium (*plural*: millennia) A period of one thousand years; also the time at the end of a thousand-year period.

philosopher A person who thinks and teaches about ideas and larger truths.

prophecy A divinely inspired statement that predicts the future.

republic A form of government in which leaders are chosen by the voting public to represent them.

ritual A fixed or standardized religious ceremony.

torque (TORK) A metal ring or band worn around the neck, put on by twisting an opening at one end.

tribe A group of people who have the same ancestors, social customs, and other characteristics.

zodiac (ZOH-dee-ak) An imaginary band in the heavens, through which the sun, moon, and planets seem to move during the year; the zodiac is divided into twelve parts, each named for a constellation.

FOR FURTHER READING

Beck, Barbara. *The First Book of the Ancient Maya*. New York: Franklin Watts, 1965.

Bianchi, Robert Steven. *The Nubians: People of the Ancient Nile*. Brookfield, CT: Millbrook Press, 1994.

Corbishley, Mike. *Ancient Rome*. New York: Facts on File, 1989.

Editors of Readers Digest. *The Mysteries of the Ancient Americas*. Pleasantville, NY: Readers Digest, 1986.

Ferron, Peggy. *China*. New York: Marshall Cavendish, 1991.

Galvin, Irene Flum. *The Ancient Maya*. New York: Marshall Cavendish, 1997.

Greenblatt, Miriam. *Alexander the Great and Ancient Greece*. New York: Marshall Cavendish, 2000.

Greene, Jacqueline Denbar. *The Maya*. New York: Franklin Watts, 1992.

Grimal, Pierre. *Stories of Alexander the Great*. Cleveland, OH: World Publishing Co., 1965.

Hartz, Paula. *Taoism*. New York: Facts on File, 1993.

Hinds, Kathryn. *The Ancient Romans*. New York: Marshall Cavendish, 1997.

————. *The Celts of Northern Europe*. New York: Marshall Cavendish, 1997.

Hoobler, Thomas, and Dorothy Hoobler. *Confucianism*. New York: Facts on File, 1993.

Lerner Publications. *India in Pictures*. Minneapolis, MN: Lerner, 1989.

MacDonald, Fiona. *The World in the Time of Alexander the Great*. Parsippany, NJ: Dillon Press, 1997.

Marston, Elsa. *The Ancient Egyptians*. New York: Marshall Cavendish, 1996.

Martell, Hazel Mary. *The Celts*. NY: Penguin Group, 1996.

McNair, Sylvia. *India*. Chicago: Childrens Press, 1990.

Morrison, Tony. *The Mystery of the Nasca Lines*. Woodbridge, Suffolk, England: Nonesuch Expeditions, 1987.

Murowchick, Robert E. *China: Ancient Cultures, Modern Land*. Norman: University of Oklahoma Press, 1994.

Nardo, Don. *The Roman Republic*. San Diego, CA: Lucent, 1994.

Robinson, Charles Alexander. *Alexander the Great: Conqueror and Creator of a New World*. New York: Franklin Watts, 1963.

Sattler, Helen Roney. *The Earliest Americans*. New York: Clarion, 1993.

Schomp, Virginia. *The Ancient Greeks*. New York: Marshall Cavendish, 1996.

Service, Pamela F. *The Ancient African Kingdom of Kush*. New York: Marshall Cavendish, 1998.

Shemie, Bonnie. *Mounds of Earth and Shell*. Toronto: Tundra Books, 1993.

Shinnie, Margaret. *Ancient African Kingdoms.*New York: St. Martin's Press, 1965.

Somerset Fry, Plantagenet. *DK History of the World*. New York: DK Publishing, 1994.

Steele, Philip. *Food & Feasts in Ancient Rome*. New York: Macmillan, 1994.

Stuart, Gene S. *America's Ancient Cities*. Washington, DC: National Geographic Society, 1988.

Stuart, George E., and Gene S. Stuart. *The Mysterious Maya*. Washington, DC: National Geographic Society, 1977.

Williams, Brian. *Ancient China*. New York: Viking, 1996.

Wood, Marion. *Ancient America*. New York: Facts on File, 1990.

ON-LINE INFORMATION*

http://www.ipl.org/youth
Index of links for different sites about
ancient civilizations and cultures.

http://www.greekciv.pdx.edu
An overview of Greek civilization with
information, maps, and related links.

http://www.sci.mus.mn.us/sln/ma/index.html
Information on Mayan culture with
photos, maps, activities, and related
links. Sponsored by the Science Museum
of Minnesota.

http://library.thinkquest.org
An assortment of on-line educational
resources about history and culture.

http://www.carthage.edu/outis/carthage.html
Photos and additional information
about Carthage.

http://www.clannada.org/docs/theline.htm
Overview of Celtic history and Gaelic
culture with links to additional on-line
Celtic resources.

http://www.wsu.edu:8080/~dee/MOD-
ULES.HTM
Excellent collection of information and
images of ancient Egypt, ancient China,
ancient Greece, ancient Rome, ancient
India, the Olmec, and the Maya.

http://clearwater.nic.edu/socsci/jasylte/Me
roecem.htm
Information and photos of Kush
and Meroë.

http://www.houseofptolemy.org
An index of links and information
about Ptolemaic Egypt as well as links
for other sites about Egypt.

*Websites change from time to time. For
additional on-line information, check with
the media specialist at your local library.*

ABOUT THE AUTHOR

Pamela Service grew up
in Berkeley, California.
From early on, she liked
reading and telling stories
set in the past—and in
possible futures. Her
published books include
two history volumes with Marshall
Cavendish and fifteen works of science
fiction and fantasy, often with history
woven through them.

After receiving a master's degree in
African history from the University of
London and working on excavations in
England and Sudan, she and her husband,
Bob, moved to Indiana where she was
curator of a history museum for seventeen
years. Now she is working as director of a
history museum in Eureka, California.

BIBLIOGRAPHY

Asimov, Isaac. *The Roman Republic*. Boston: Houghton Mifflin, 1966.

Bevan, Edwyn. *The House of Ptolemy*. Chicago: Argonaut, 1968.

Cremin, Aedeen. *The Celts*. New York: Rizzoli, 1997.

Ellis, Walter M. *Ptolemy of Egypt*. London: Routledge, 1994.

Fairbank, John. *China: A New History*. Cambridge, MA: Harvard University Press, 1992.

Freidel, David, Linda Schele, and Joy Parker. *Maya Cosmos: Three Thousand Years on the Shaman's Path*. New York: William Morrow, 1993.

Grainger, John D. *Seleukos Nikator*. New York: Routledge, 1990.

Hammond, N. G. L. *The Genius of Alexander the Great*. Chapel Hill: University of North Carolina Press, 1997.

Hammond, N. G. L., and H. H. Scullard, eds. *The Oxford Classical Dictionary*. Oxford: Oxford University Press, 1970.

Huang, Ray. *China: A Macro History*. Armonk, NY: M. E. Sharpe, 1989.

Kruta, Venceslas, and Werner Forman. *The Celts of the West*. London: Orbis, 1985.

Kublin, Hyman. *China*. Boston: Houghton Mifflin, 1968.

Lumbrerus, Luis G. *The Peoples and Cultures of Ancient Peru*. Washington, DC: Smithsonian Institution Press, 1974.

Macedo, Justo Caceres. *The Prehispanic Cultures of Peru*. Lima: Perugraph, 1988.

McDonald, A. H. *Republican Rome*. New York: Praeger, 1966.

McEvedy, Colin. *The Penguin Atlas of African History*. New York: Penguin Books, 1995.

Mercer, Charles. *Alexander the Great*. New York: American Heritage, 1962.

Morrison, Tony. *Pathways to the Gods: The Mystery of the Andes Lines*. New York: Harper and Row, 1978.

Nilakanta, Sastri K. A. *Age of the Nandas and Mauryas*. Banaras, India: Motilal Banarsidass, 1952.

O'Faolain, Eileen. *Irish Sagas and Folk-tales*. London: Oxford University Press, 1954.

Paranavitana, Senarat. *The Greeks and the Mauryas*. Colombo, Ceylon: Lake House, 1971.

Paul, Anne, ed. *Paracas Art & Architecture*. Iowa City: University of Iowa Press, 1991.

Picard, Gilbert Charles, and Colette Picard. *Daily Life in Carthage.* New York: Macmillan, 1966.

———. *The Life and Death of Carthage.* New York: Taplinger, 1968.

Rogerson, Barnaby. *A Traveler's History of North Africa.* New York: Interlink Books, 1998.

Sattler, Helen Roney. *The Earliest Americans.* New York: Clarion, 1993.

Schele, Linda, and David Freidel. *A Forest of Kings: The Untold Story of the Ancient Maya.* New York: William Morrow, 1990.

Shinnie, Peter. *Meroë, A Civilization of the Sudan.* London: Thames and Hudson, 1967.

Smith, Vincent. *The Early History of India.* Oxford: Clarendon Press, 1962.

Snow, Dean. *The Archaeology of North America.* New York: Viking, 1976.

Soren, David, Aicha Ben Abed Ben Khader, and Hedi Slim. *Carthage: Uncovering the Mysteries and Splendors of Ancient Tunisia.* New York: Simon and Schuster, 1990.

Tripathni, Ramashankar. *The History of Ancient India.* Delhi, India: Motilal Banarsidass, 1942.

Walbank, F. W. *The Helenistic World.* Atlantic Highlands, NJ: Humanities Press, 1981.

Welsby, Derek. *The Kingdom of Kush.* Princeton, NJ: Marcus Wiener Publishers, 1998.

Woodcock, George. *The Greeks in India.* London: Faber and Faber, 1966.

INDEX

*Page numbers for illustrations are
in boldface.*

Adena people, 82–83, 85, 87
Africa, 29, 33
    the Carthaginians, 26, 29, 34–39, **35**, **36–37**, **38**
    the Egyptians, 15–16, 40–43, **40**, **41**, **42**, **43**
    the Kushites, 44–47, **45**, **47**
    map of, **32**
    Nok people, 48, **49**, 50–51, **51**
Alexander the Great, 7, 10, **11**, 12–17, **12**, **14–15**, **16**, **17**,
    21, 26, 29, 37, 40–41, 43, 53, 54, 55, 58
Alexandria, Egypt, **6**, 17, 41, **41**, 42, **42**, 43, **43**
Americas, the, 69
    map of, **68**
    the Mesoamericans, 70–75, **71**, **72**, **74**
    the North Americans, 82–87, **83**, **84–85**, **86**
    the South Americans, 76–81, **77**, **78**, **80**
Amon (god), 44
animal sacrifices, 36
animals
    boars, 21
    guinea pigs, 81
    livestock, 81
Antigonus the One Eyed, 54, 55, 56
Antiochus, 60
Apama, 57
Apamea, ruins of, **55**
Apedemek, 47
Apicius, 31
Appian Way, 28
Appius Claudius Caecus, 27–29, **29**
aqueduct, Roman, 28
Arakamani, 44
Aristotle, **12**, 13, 43
armies
    Carthaginian army, 37
    Chinese, 64, **64**
    Egyptian army, 41
    Roman army, 29–30, **30**
Arsinoë II, **40**
Asia, 53
    the Chinese, 62–67, **63**, **64**, **66**, **67**
    the Indians, 55, 58–61, **59**
    map of, **52**
    the Persians, 15, 54–57, **54**, **55**
astronomer, **6**

Ba'al Hamon (god), 34
Babylon, 54, 56
bards, 22
Berbers, the, 35
Bernice (daughter of Seleucus I), 58, 60
Bindusara, 60
bronze, 21
Bucephalus (horse), 7, 10, **11**, 12, 17
burial mounds, 82

calendars, 72, 74
caravans, 38
Carthaginians, the, 26, 29, 34–39, **35**, **36–37**, **38**
catapults, 29
Celts, the, 15, 18–25, **19**, **20**, **23**, **24**, **25**, 26, 48
Chandragupta Maurya, 55, 58, **59**
chariots, **14–15**, **19**
child sacrifice, 34, 36, 37
Ch'in dynasty, 62, **63**, 64, **64**, 65, 67
Ch'in Shih Huangti, **63**, 64–66, **64**
Chinese, the, 62–67, **63**, **64**, **66**, **67**
city-states, Greek, 14, 29
clay figures, 48, **49**, **64**
clothing, Celtic, 24–25, **25**
cloths, woven, 77, **77**, **78**
Confucianism, 66, 67
Confucius, 65–67
cooking baskets, 86, **86**
Cuchullin, 18, **19**, 20
culture, Roman, 26–27
currency
    cacao beans used as, 75
    Greek coins, **17**
    Persian coins, **54**

Darius III, **14–15**
democracy, 27
Dido, 35, **35**
Druids, 18, 22
    New Year's ceremony, **20**
dynasty, 57, 62, 67

Egyptians, the, 15–16, 40–43, **40**, **41**, **42**, **43**, 44
    Kushites and, **45**, 47
Eighteen Rabbit (king), 75
elephants, Indian war, 16, 30, **30**, 47, 55, 58
Etruscans, 26
Europe, 9
    the Celts, 15, 18–25, **19**, **20**, **23**, **24**, **25**, 26
    the Greeks, 10–17, **11**, **12**, **14**, **15–16**, **17**, 26
    map of, **8**
    the Romans, 21, 25, 26–31, **27**, **28**, **29**, **30**

farming
    Celtic farmers, 22
    Mayan farmers, 73
food
    cocoa, 75
    cooking baskets, 86, **86**
    Indian, 60, 61
    Roman feasts, 31

games
    in Africa, 50–51, **51**
    Mayan ball games, 70, **72**, 74, 75
glossary, 89
gods and goddesses, 34, 41, 43, 44, 47, 56, 70, **71**, 73

government
    Carthage's, 37
    Roman, 27–28
Grave Creek Mound, **83**
Greeks, the, 10–17, **11**, **12**, **14**, **15**, **16**, **17**, 26
    Carthage's war with, 36–37
    Egyptians and, 43
    Indians and, 58, 60

Hannibal, 21, **30**
Hanno, 37
Hero Twins, 70, 73
hieroglyphs, 46, 47
history books, Mayan, 74–75
Hopewell people, 87
Horus (god), 41
human sacrifices, 73–74, **74**
    child sacrifice, 34, 36, 37

Iarbus, 35
Ice Age, 69
Indians, the, 16, 55, 58–61, **59**
iron smelting, 47, 48
iron tools and weapons, 20–21, 48
Isis (goddess), 43

Jefferson, Thomas, 82
jewelry, Celtic, 22, 24, **24**

Kushites, the, 44–47, **45**, **47**

land bridges, 69
languages
    Bantu, 48
    Meroitic, 46, 47
Lao-tzu, 65, **67**
Legalism, 67
Library of Alexandria, 43, **43**
lighthouses, 42, **42**, 43
line drawings, ancient, 79–80, **80**
Lords of Death, 70

Macedon, 10, 11, 12–13, 41
Macedonian School of Pages, 13, 40, 54
Mancala (game), 50
mathematics, 74
Maya, the, 72–75, **72**, **74**
Mediterranean Sea, 22, 34, 42
mercenaries, 58
merchants, seafaring, 37–38
Meroë, city of, 44–45, 47
Mesoamericans, the, 70–75, **71**, **72**, **74**
metalwork, 24, **24**, **25**, 48
Miwok Indians, 86
mounds, earthen, 82, **83**, **84–85**, 85, 87
mummies, 76–77, **77**

Napata, city of, 44
Native Americans, early, 82
Nazca people, 79–80, **80**
Nok people, 48, **49**, 50–51, **51**
North Americans, the, 82–87, **83**, **84–85**, **86**

Olmec people, 70, **71**, 72, 74
Olympias, 13
Osiris (god), 41, 43

Paracas people, 76–79, **77**, **78**
Period of Warring States, 62, 63, 65
Persians, the, 15, 54–57, **54**, **55**
Peru, ancient, 76–81
Pharology, 42
Pharos lighthouse, 42, **42**, 43
Philip of Macedon, 10, 11
philosophers, 13, 43, 60, 65, 67
Phoenicians, the, 34
Pits and Pebbles (game), 50–51, **51**
pottery, 86, **86**, 87
prophesies, 13
Ptolemy II, 21, 40–41, **40**, 42, 43, 54, 57
pyramids, 45, **47**, **72**, 73, 76
Pyrrhus, 30

religion, Celtic, 22
Richard III, 21
Romans, the, 21, 25, 26–31, **27**, **28**, **29**, **30**
    Carthaginians and, **38**, 39
    Egyptians and, 43
Romulus and Remus, **28**

Sahara Desert, 33, 38, 48
Sarapis (god), 43
Seleucus I, 54–57, **54**, 58
Senate, Roman, 27, **30**
Serpent Mound, **84–85**
Seven Wonders of the World, 42
siege towers, 29
"slash and burn" agriculture, 73
Sostratus, 42
South Americans, the, 76–81, **77**, **78**, **80**
sports, 61, 70, **72**, 74, 75
stoneworkers, 70, **71**, 72

Tanit (goddess), 34
Taoism, 65–67
Tiber River, 26, 28, 29
torques, 24, **24**
Tyre, city of, 15, 34, 35, 37

Vikings, 21

war clubs, 77
weapons, 77
women
    Celtic, 22
    Indian warriors, 61
world events around 300 B.C., 88
World Tree, 73
writing
    invention of, 33
    Mayan writing system, 74
    Meroitic writing system, 46, 47
    Olmec writing system, 72

yin-yang, 66, **66**

Zeus, 56
Zhuangzi, 66